Subodh Gupta

The imaginary order of things
El orden imaginario de las cosas

CAC MÁLAGA
CENTRO DE ARTE CONTEMPORÁNEO DE MÁLAGA

5 JULIO - 13 OCTUBRE 2013
5 JULY - 13 OCTOBER 2013

cacmálaga Centro de Arte
Contemporáneo de Málaga

Ayuntamiento de Málaga

AYUNTAMIENTO DE MÁLAGA

Francisco de la Torre Prados
Alcalde

Damián Caneda
Concejal de Cultura, Juventud y Deportes

Susana Martín
Directora del Área de Cultura, Educación y Turismo

María Teresa Barrau
Secretaria de la Comisión

CAC MÁLAGA

Fernando Francés
Director

Mª José García
Gerencia

Marta Taboada
Adjunta Dirección

Helena Juncosa
Alicia Gutiérrez
Exposiciones

Victoria Ruiz
Natalia Motta
Actividades Culturales

Ester García
Biblioteca

Inés Fernández
Pilar Díaz
Virginia Illana
Actividades Pedagógicas

Gema Chamizo
Sara Guerra
Alberto Ricca
Joaquín Alarcón
Comunicación e Imagen

Mihail E. Plesanu
Fernando Sarria
Departamento Técnico

Alicia Bustamante
Administración

cacmálaga Centro de Arte
Contemporáneo de Málaga

Alemania, s/n. 29001 Málaga.
Tel. +34 952 12 00 55. Fax: +34 952 21 01 77
cacmalaga@cacmalaga.eu
www.cacmalaga.org

EXPOSICIÓN

Fernando Francés
Comisario

Helena Juncosa
Gestión Cultural y Comunicación, S. L.
Organización y Coordinación

Mihail E. Plesanu
Fernando Sarria
Lukas Willem
Prateek
Factum Arte
Moisés Berubel
Carlo Cervantes
Francisco Jiménez
José Mª Marfil
José Andrés Navarro
Antonio Núñez
Javier Ruiz
Montaje

TDM. Transportes y Montajes de Arte, S. L.
InteArt
Universal Art Relocation Team
Transporte

Nationale Suisse
Seguro

CATÁLOGO

Fernando Francés
Subodh Gupta
Textos

Alberto Ricca
Diseño

Laura E. Suffield
Discobole, S. L.
Traducción

Stefan Altenburger Photography Zürich
Mike Bruce
Alan Dimmick
Alex Delfanne
José Luis Gutiérrez
Jussi Koivunen
Thomas Müller
Dominique Uldry
Fotografía

Imprenta J. Martínez, S. L.
Impresión

ISBN: 978-84-940836-5-5

Depósito Legal: SA-422-2013

© de las obras, Subodh Gupta
© de los textos y de las fotografías, sus autores
© de la edición, Gestión Cultural y Comunicación, S. L. – CAC Málaga

AGRADECIMIENTOS

Maria Brassel
Angelika Felder
Emil Guggenbühl
James Lavender
Julia Lenz
Prateek
Sanjana Sarkar
Michel Studerus
Iwan & Manuela Wirth

Nuestro agradecimiento muy especial
a Subodh Gupta y a la galería Hauser & Wirth sin cuyo apoyo,
implicación y entusiasmo esta exposición
no hubiera sido posible.

Índice | Contents

FRANCISCO DE LA TORRE PRADOS | Alcalde de Málaga

El Centro de Arte Contemporáneo de Málaga presenta la exposición *Subodh Gupta. El orden imaginario de las cosas*, la primera muestra individual de este artista indio en España. Está compuesta por diecinueve de obras, esculturas, instalaciones y un vídeo. Algunas de estas piezas son inéditas.

Una seña de identidad de Subodh Gupta es que transmite la cultura de su país desde un prisma y una perspectiva completamente diferentes a la visión de los medios o el cine. Utensilios y objetos cotidianos, usados en el día a día de cualquier familia de la India son la materia prima de su trabajo, además del empleo de una diversidad de materiales, como son la madera, el bronce o el mármol.

La unión entre tradición y modernidad, su interpretación de la religión, a través de la importancia que le da a los alimentos, y rituales de su país se muestran en el trabajo de este artista desde un punto de vista único y con el empleo de una estética contemporánea, alejada de cualquier estereotipo o cliché cultural.

Una vez más, la propuesta expositiva del CAC Málaga es una oportunidad única para contemplar el trabajo de uno de los artistas internacionales más importantes del momento actual. Además, es otro ejemplo del firme compromiso del Centro por situar a Málaga como referente del arte contemporáneo en todo el mundo.

Subodh Gupta, el efecto poético de los objetos y la memoria

FERNANDO FRANCÉS | Director del CAC Málaga

Desde la aparición del Homo sapiens, que fue capaz de pintar la cueva de Altamira en el Magdaleniense, incluso mucho antes, el hombre ha tratado de explicar en los procesos creativos aquellos aspectos de lo físico y lo espiritual que, o bien le preocupaban para consolidar su propia existencia, o no entendían, en este caso afanándose en la búsqueda de respuestas a sus dudas, verdaderamente imaginativas.

Una característica común a todos esos procesos de exploración, es la dimensión global de su interpretación. El arte tiene la peculiaridad de ser un lenguaje comprensible a la mirada de la mayoría de los ojos con independencia del idioma que hable el sujeto que mira, con las obvias limitaciones en el terreno conceptual del nivel cultural de éste. Incluso el arte de la representación, o el jeroglífico, pueda ser comprensible para individuos que vivan miles de años después.

Por otra parte, el arte es capaz de trasmitir los mensajes en forma de compromiso y poesía, y ambos igualmente, son fácilmente accesibles para una gran mayoría en un mundo tan globalizado como este. Para llegar a un grado alto de interacción quizá sea necesario captar los matices, conocer los detalles del entorno social en el que el arte ha sido creado, pero en cualquier caso y aún con la libre interpretación del espectador, el arte puede llegar a trasmitir sensaciones y mensajes comprensibles para todos. No es mi pretensión afirmar que el arte es comunicación, aunque también pueda serlo de forma colateral, sino que esa no es su primera función, su razón de ser. Lo que sí me parece más que necesario, incluso constituyente, es la capacidad del arte para la reflexión sobre la vida, sobre el hecho humano y las causas y consecuencias de sus relaciones y acciones, y creo también, sinceramente, que el que no desarrolla esa capacidad, se ha quedado absolutamente obsoleto.

El arte que nace de la experiencia, de la realidad social, política, económica y cultural, del debate del mundo actual, de la no complacencia, está más dotado de pureza y fundamento y, al tiempo, esa sobredosis le confiere mucha más autenticidad y credibilidad. Lo opuesto sería el arte que se define sólo como belleza con una intencionalidad exclusivamente estética. El arte se reinventa cada día y el de la actualidad no puede ser ajeno a lo que acontece en el mundo, a interpretar los procesos sociológicos, intelectuales e incluso medioambientales que estamos padeciendo. Y es muy evidente la capacidad de conexión que genera el que tiene como punto de partida ese hecho humano. La clave está en hacerlo de diferente manera, reinventando los procesos creativos, añadiéndoles puntos de vista novedosos que aporten originales maneras de entender lo que parece ya inventado. Y en esa búsqueda de lo distinto, la experiencia vivida por el artista de diferentes lugares y culturas, la biografía de cada uno, es un aspecto fundamental para lograrla. Lo otro sería que el artista volviera a refugiarse en una urna de cristal impasible e insensible a lo que acontece fuera de ella. Las torres de marfil que separan de la realidad al artista con el mundo son cada vez más anacrónicas y el arte que surge de ellas pierde el componente de responsabilidad y compromiso que se requiere para que pueda llegar a emocionar.

Paradójicamente los agentes del arte, los comisarios y los responsables de las programaciones de los museos principalmente, quizá en un alarde corporativista, han ido con los años mediatizando la acción creativa, redirigiéndola en su conjunto, seleccionando sólo aquellas acciones que pudieran tener una concepción homogénea y proscribiendo todo tipo de arte que surge desde la independencia y la libertad. Pocos son los artistas que escapan a ese control de los críticos y comisarios, quienes entienden en su gran mayoría que el arte no debe emocionar sino únicamente ser consecuencia de un pensamiento político o un proceso histórico e, instrumentalmente, intelectual. Pero lo cierto es que el pensamiento y el compromiso sin la emoción quedan huérfanos, y casi con total seguridad, también quedarán olvidados en el tiempo.

Lo cierto es que, a medida que avanzan los años, me resulta más difícil encontrar en una misma obra de arte, en un mismo artista, todas esas razones de autenticidad y verdad. El mundo se ha ido progresivamente trivializando, y el arte no ha sido ajeno a ese proceso. Paseas por exposiciones y por los pasillos de las ferias buscando algo que te conmueva y a veces es frustrante no hallarlo y tienes la sensación de que muchos artistas viven y producen su obra desde los parámetros y criterios de los agentes y desde su propia idiosincrasia personal, ocultando su auténtico pensamiento libre. Echo mucho en falta una libertad de creación tanto como la libertad de cátedra que se exige en la universidad. Y quizá por eso, y reconociendo que el nivel cultural de la población aumenta en todos los lugares de forma notable, aún en el arte contemporáneo está muy alejado de la gente real que es reacia a no querer entenderlo pese a ser plausible dicha comprensión.

Hace ya unos años, paseando por una de esas ferias cada vez más anodinas y previsibles, quedé abducido por una exquisita composición de objetos de metal brillantes ordenados cuidadosamente en círculo, platos y cubiertos que flotaban en el aire sujetos por unos finos hilos de nailon desde el techo en un equilibrio inquietante. El aire de las personas en movimiento junto a la instalación hacía que las piezas se movieran lentamente, incluso el aire acondicionado afectaba a la frágil quietud de los objetos. La primera impresión fue causa de una atracción estética que duró unos pocos minutos. Enseguida aquella obra hablaba e intentaba llamar la atención sobre otras consideraciones que se escapaban a una rápida e inmediata mirada. Pese a que el lugar no era el más indicado para la obra, pese a que la mayoría de la gente pasaba sin apenas detenerse en aquella pequeña instalación, pese a su aparente modestia... una carga de profundidad había explotado en mi interior, no sé si en el cerebro, en la médula, en el corazón o en el estómago, o quizá estalló en todos esos sitios a la vez.

Había visto, obviamente antes, otras obras de Subodh Gupta en varias ocasiones. Recuerdo, a bote pronto, en el Palais de Tokyo o en la 51 ª Bienal de Venecia donde se presentó la obra *Curry,* 2005, antecedente directo de *Take off your shoes and wash your hands*, 2008, instalación que ahora se presenta en el CAC Málaga, pero nunca antes me habían causado un efecto semejante. Es extraño cómo funcionan los resortes, los vínculos entre la mirada y el cerebro. O quizá es una cuestión de predisposición, de conexión intelectual, de coincidir en un mismo segmento de intere-

ses y preocupaciones. Lo cierto es que aquella obra incentivó no sólo mi interés por el artista sino también por la India. Mi relación con este país se limitaba hasta ese momento básicamente a una serie de artículos que escribí en mi juventud, siendo objetor de conciencia, sobre Mahatma Gandhi y la no violencia.

Una de mis preocupaciones y constantes personales en el mundo del arte ha sido siempre buscar artistas cuya obra me emocionase especialmente, y cuando esa situación se ha producido —casos tan dispares como los de William Kentridge, Lawrence Weiner, Tracey Emin, Raymond Pettibon o Ai Weiwei— uno tiene la seguridad de que el arte es, sin duda, una de las pocas medicinas capaz de sanar las enfermedades del mundo y al tiempo de serenar las tormentas interiores, neutralizando a los mons-

Take off your shoes and wash your hands, 2008 (detalle / detail)
Tramway, Glasgow, Escocia / Scotland, 2010
Cortesía el artista y Hauser & Wirth / Courtesy the artist and Hauser & Wirth
Foto / Photo: Alan Dimmick

truos del subconsciente. Esa experiencia la he vivido en los últimos años con cada obra que, de Subodh Gupta, se tropezaba en mi camino. Y mi fascinación ante sus ideas, su obra y su posición como artista ha ido creciendo sistemáticamente sin descanso.

Hay en Gupta un aspecto que confiere credibilidad máxima a su trabajo y que, por ende, no es demasiado frecuente, como una declaración de principios, entre otros artistas principalmente de su generación. Me refiero a su interés por reflexionar sobre el entorno próximo. En él encontró el joven artista, al inicio de su carrera, las claves para inventar un territorio artístico propio. El artista ha comentado la importancia que tuvo para él aquella incipiente instalación de 29 taburetes que realizó en la Sanskriti Kendra de Delhi donde residía con otros artistas. Y esa obra abrió el camino a un mundo fascinante de imágenes y recuerdos de la infancia. De esta manera, su experiencia personal se convirtió en la primera fuente de alimentación de su pensamiento y también el carácter diferenciador de su trabajo, algo que siempre ha sido un destino buscado por el artista en un ejercicio que considero muy necesario actualmente y que tiene que ver con la voluntad de no seguir los criterios, formas y temas *oficiales*. De su infancia se reencontró con la atracción que para él tenía la cocina y la afición por el manejo del menaje al cocinar. Los utensilios, las herramientas, que se usan en la cocina tenían para él una fascinación especial. La aparición del acero en el escenario cocina, no sólo era un signo de progreso de una incipiente sociedad media sino también un símbolo de evidencia de la citada evolución. Por otra parte, el metal representa, frente a la madera o la cerámica, un avance tecnológico muy radical, con lo que supone de mejora en la resistencia de los objetos así como en la mejora de la higiene. Ese mismo recuerdo que el artista tiene de este periodo y lo que suponía esa cierta atracción por la cocina no es un hecho en sí mismo diferenciador de la India. Puedo recordar de mi infancia en la España de los sesenta ese mismo sentimiento. La cocina marcaba el orden de la vida y los útiles de metal colgaban de una barra que se ponía en la cocina, no sólo para que se pudiera acceder a ellos con facilidad sino como un emblema de modernidad, como

Untitled, 2011
Acero inoxidable y cobre / Stainless steel, copper
264,2 x 152,4 x 152,4 cm
Panorámica / Installation view *Subodh Gupta. A glass of water*,
Hauser & Wirth, Nueva York / New York, 2011
Cortesía el artista y Hauser & Wirth / Courtesy the artist and Hauser & Wirth
Foto / Photo: Thomas Müller

un símbolo de lujo y decoración. Y cuando veo sus bicicletas y motos con perolas colgando del manillar o sujetas en los laterales no puedo menos que recordar que de esa misma manera iba de niño desde la casa de la playa al pueblo a buscar la leche fresca cada tarde. Y compruebo que algo semejante pasaba en su casa del *Tebsil* de Bilhar donde vivió su niñez. Es curioso que sea un artista indio, de un país tan lejano y una cultura tan diferente, quien te ayude a recordar tu propia infancia y juventud, rememorando él la suya.

Repose, 2001
Acero inoxidable / Stainless steel
73,7 x 259,1 x 127 cm
Panorámica / Installation view
Subodh Gupta. A glass of water, Hauser & Wirth,
Nueva York / New York, 2011
Cortesía el artista y Hauser & Wirth /
Courtesy the artist and Hauser & Wirth
Foto / Photo: Thomas Müller

Con el tiempo, el menaje de metal se ha convertido no sólo en los elementos que constituyen una obra total y compleja, las piezas que completan la visión de un todo, sino la propia materia prima con la que se define la simbología, el material y el mensaje. Coexisten en las obras de Gupta dicotomías permanentes que enfrentan las dos mitades de su acción y su pensamiento. De esa manera dialogan continuamente entre sí obras que, basadas en recuerdos e imágenes de la vida cotidiana de cualquier ciudad o aldea india, reflejan conscientemente un cierto desorden y caos que traslada al espectador de la obra a la parte más endémica de la tradición india popular (*Ancestor Cupboard* 2012, *216 Sacks*, 2012, *Season*, 2013, *Two Cows*, 2003-2008, o incluso *All in the same boat*, 2012-2013, con otras caracterizadas por el orden, el equilibrio, la frialdad metódica de los procesos propios de un tiempo postindustrial y de influencia minimal (*School*, 2008), *Take off your shoes and wash your hands*, 2008 o *Faith Matters*, 2007-2008).

Colony, 2013
36 fiambreras tiffin lacadas / 36 lacquered tiffins
Dimensiones variables / Variable dimensions
Cortesía el artista y Hauser & Wirth / Courtesy the artist and Hauser & Wirth
Foto / Photo: Alex Delfanne

Gupta indaga en lo más superficial de la vida india, en el álbum de su iconografía más reconocible y visible, para profundizar en los significados de una evolución social apabullante y compleja. Sin embargo, en absoluto puede entenderse su obra como un compromiso político, como el arte resultado de una acción política tan del gusto de algunos comisarios posmodernos. Él se limita a trascribir una realidad concreta por él conocida y vivida a un idioma universal. La globalidad de cierto tipo de arte que se construye desde el sentimiento permite que sus recuerdos, como un diario de emociones, sean comprensibles para un público heterogéneo y diverso. Y esa capacidad expansiva es al tiempo una de las singularidades del artista. Él buscaba hacer un tipo de arte diferente, era casi una obsesión, pero al tiempo de conseguir el yacimiento de su ideas consiguió también que fueran diferentes los códigos de lectura de su intención. Y es ahí precisamente donde reside la faceta más conceptual de su proceso creativo. Gupta vive y trabaja en Nueva Delhi, lo cual confiere credibilidad a su pensamiento y contribuye a que su obra no sea algo ajeno a su vida cotidiana. Igual que ocurre con Ai Weiwei en Pekín o Kentridge en Johannesburgo, Gupta es de los contados artistas que no han sucumbido al éxito de su trabajo en occidente y, por ende, han abandonado el origen conceptual de su obra y su pensamiento, íntimamente ligado a su lugar de residencia. Y es de ahí desde donde el artista construye un compendio de ideas que aluden a un mensaje, unas veces poético o tras vulgar, pero que en ambos casos contribuyen a formatear un discurso sobre su propia historia y la de su país. Y como venía explicando, pese a trabajar desde el centro neurálgico de la cultura india, en la obra de Gupta aparecen referencias continuas a la historia del arte contemporáneo occidental, no tanto en la formalidad sino en una especie de *apropiacionismo* al servicio de su propio proceso de creación. Si en las obras donde busca una inmersión en la tradición rastreando materiales antiguos, ya sean útiles de cocina, recipientes, instrumentos musicales o una simple pirámide de sacos (*Cosmic Jewel,* 2012), la apariencia resulta una especie de conglomerado

Line of Control, 2008
Estructura de acero y acero inoxidable y utensilios de acero inoxidable
Stainless steal and steel structure, stainless steel utensils /
1000 x 1000 x 1000 cm
Cortesía el artista y Hauser & Wirth / Courtesy the artist and Hauser & Wirth
Foto / Photo: Mike Bruce

povera, en otras, el sentimiento, que no la influencia, es realmente minimal (*Untitled,* 2008, o *Faith* Matters, 2007-2008), conceptual (*Oil on canvas,* 2010, o *A glass of water,* 2011) o incluso en muchas ocasiones su obra pudiera ser concebida como un *ready-made* (*216 Sacks*, 2012) ya que muchas veces los materiales son encontrados en el mismo lugar donde vive. En cualquier caso Gupta, ya sea recodificando un objeto, reproduciéndolo en

Gandhi's Three Monkeys, 2007-2008
Bronce, utensilios viejos y acero /
Bronze, old utensils, steel
Cabeza con máscara de gas / Gas mask head:
184 x 140 x 256 cm
Cabeza con pasamontañas / Balaclava head:
200 x 131 x 155 cm
Cabeza con casco / Helmet head:
175 x 125 x 150 cm
Cortesía el artista y Hauser & Wirth /
Courtesy the artist and Hauser & Wirth
to / Photo: Stefan Altenburger Photography Zürich

acero o bronce, o usándolo tal cual ha sido comprado o encontrado y creando una realidad nueva a partir de una idea, ha conseguido inventar una nueva manera de escribir una autobiografía que fluye veracidad y sentimiento.

Su obra no es ajena al compromiso con el entorno no sólo cultural y religioso sino también geográfico. La instalación *Renunciation,* 2012, basada en la reproducción del conjunto monumental de los Budas de Bamiyán en Afganistán después de ser destruido por el régimen de los ayatolas, es un claro ejemplo. A través de unos pequeños agujeros se puede ver en el interior de esta montaña sagrada para los budistas, un conjunto de reliquias de la ausencia. Buda, al igual que los ermitaños de Meteora en Tesalia y los de tantos otros lugares, renunció a todos los privilegios materiales para vivir meditando en soledad y alcanzar el estado de *Budeidad* desde el que pudiera liberar a todos los hombres que sufrían. Contrasta aquí nuevamente una de las dicotomías aludidas anteriormente. Si los objetos de metal que atiborran las esculturas e instalaciones de Gupta, bandejas, cacerolas, perolas, platos, cubiertos, tazas, calderos, ollas, vasos, cuencos, lozas..., muestran de alguna manera, no sólo el estilo de vida sino la evolución burguesa de las clases medias de la India y la aspiración a conseguir un mayor nivel, esta obra representa uno de los conceptos más arraigados del hinduismo: la necesidad de vivir sin

1 KG WAR, 2007
1 kg de oro / 1 kg gold
Cortesía el artista y Hauser & Wirth /
Courtesy the artist and Hauser & Wirth

nada para alcanzar la pureza. Hay que recordar que Gupta no es ahora practicante de ninguna religión y por tanto su compromiso es el de un espectador que ha vivido la experiencia pero que la relata con la distancia del tiempo y se aprecia una cierta lejanía emocional en la forma de exponer su visión sobre el tema cuando este tiene un origen religioso o político. Su opción real, su apuesta individual es solo con el arte y ahí nuevamente se distingue una voluntad de compromiso con el proceso creativo que aúna filosofía y proceso. Aunque el conflicto bélico de Afganistán no tiene relación

con esa obra, la guerra, la violencia o que la India sea uno de los países que poseen una capacidad nuclear si aparece más que sutilmente en su trabajo (*Line of Control,* 2008, *Gandhi's Three Monkeys*, 2008 o *1 K.G. WAR*, 2007).

Bullet, 2007
Latón y cromo / Brass, chrome
Tamaño real / Life size
Cortesía / Courtesy Nature Morte, Nueva Delhi / New Delhi

¿Qué madre no le ha dicho a su hijo, al menos cuando los niños no jugaban casi exclusivamente con videojuegos o con el ordenador, aquello de "quítate los zapatos y lávate las manos antes de comer"? Los recuerdos infantiles son, al parecer, iguales en cualquier parte del mundo. Hay una dosis verdaderamente importante de ironía y sentido del humor en la actitud artística de Gupta, en muchas de sus obras y sin duda en muchos de sus títulos (*Gandhi's Three Monkeys,* 2008 o *Family Nest No 3,* 2012, donde un conjunto armónico y compacto de objetos semejantes se ve de repente rodeado por otros de diferentes formas, colores y orígenes, agarrándose como buenamente pueden, colgando de las esquinas y situándose en la periferia de ese núcleo central original que es como realmente crecen las

Doot, 2003
Aluminio / Aluminium
170 x 163 x 420 cm
Subodh Gupta, Sara Hildén Art Museum, Tampere, Finlandia / Finland, 2011
Cortesía el artista y Hauser & Wirth / Courtesy the artist and Hauser & Wirth
Foto / Photo: Jussi Koivunen

Cheap Rice, 2006
Rickshaw tamaño real, utensilios de latón y metal /
Life size rickshaw, brass utensils, metal
170 x 120 x 280 cm
Cortesía el artista / Courtesy the artist

What does the vessel contain, that the river does not, 2012
Técnica mixta / Mixed media
2135 x 315 x 110 cm
Subodh Gupta. What does the vessel contain, that the river does not,
Hauser & Wirth, Londres / London, 2013
Cortesía el artista y Hauser & Wirth / Courtesy the artist and Hauser & Wirth
Foto / Photo: Alex Delfanne

familias en la realidad). Además ese mismo espíritu que trasmite en su vida cotidiana, en su forma de ser, supone también una advertencia al espectador. Es algo así como una llamada de atención para prevenirle de que "¡cuidado! Esto no es algo muy serio". Quizá esa actitud de permanente controversia, de ambigüedad y contradicción también contribuyó en aquel juego de seducción en el que me vi atrapado ya hace años con su trabajo.

La fascinación del niño Gupta no sólo fue con los objetos domésticos propios de la cocina, también la tuvo con el transporte y, para ser preciso, con las máquinas que para ello sirven. Bicicletas (*Cow,* 2005, o *Two Cows,* 2003-2008), triciclos (*Cheap Rice,* 2006), motocicletas (*Bullet,* 2006-2007), coches (*Doot,* 2003) o barcos (*What does the vessel contain, that the river does* not, 2012) están presentes continuamente en su obra. Unas veces cargan con cacerolas y perolas reviviendo la actividad cotidiana de la vida en la India, el valor del movimiento o de representación pues el artista ha definido, por ejemplo, las bicicletas como las vacas mecanizadas de la ciudad, la necesidad de trasladar agua, leche o aceites, el símbolo de posición o prosperidad de los ricos, el status, representado por el tipo de vehículo y por las perolas que no van cargadas sino de espiritualidad, muchas veces a cambio sólo de unas rupias. Por otra parte, están los coches y carros repletos de maletas y bultos (*Everything is Inside,* 2004) que trasladan su preocupación a la continua emigración de la población india, desde el país a otros lugares del mundo o desde las áreas rurales a la ciudad. Pero la migración no sólo es cuestión de objetos sino del espíritu, del alma, del pensamiento y de la cultura. Un peso demasiado importante como para prescindir de casi todo en esos procesos transitivos, que no sólo son un viaje por la geografía del planeta, sino por la del interior de cada uno. Subodh Gupta es posiblemente el artista más poético del mundo. Sin renunciar a lo material, muy al contrario, basándose en él hasta los límites de la exageración y la monumentalidad (*Bombaysers de Lille*, un homenaje a la memoria del tsunami de 2004), del barroquismo, consigue que la emoción, un sentimiento tan íntimo como escaso, entremezcla y derrumba todos los límites y los muros del pensamiento y la razón. Él es una especie de Robin Hood moderno que se apropia del drama indio, lo recodifica, lo dota de una carga emocional y lo devuelve como un regalo para los ojos y el pensamiento. Nada escapa a la casualidad en su obra. El mismo proceso de pensamiento es un rito, una ceremonia en la que, como un alquimista avezado, recupera todos los recuerdos de la infancia y la juventud, los símbolos, las cazuelas como si fueran objetos de deseo o de culto o, ambas cosas a la vez, las pátinas con mensaje, los bronces y los oros de lo sagrado, el metal aceroso del progreso industrial y todos para que el resultado sea una suerte equilibrada de antigüedad y vanguardia, de caos y orden, de equilibrio y turbación, de emoción y suspense. Sólo la habilidad de un poeta puede armonizar todos esos elementos en una obra de arte con la seguridad de que no hay mentira alguna en su discurso. La capacidad de convencer que posee la obra de Gupta es solo posible gracias al compromiso vital que el artista tiene con su obra. Uno constituye al otro como el espíritu y la materia constituyen al hombre. Complace la cualidad de este artista visionario, para acercar valores, ritos, costumbres y hábitos de oriente a una sensibilidad occidental y conseguirlo hasta el punto de la emoción. Tradicionalmente, en la cultura occidental, el brillo es desde el Renacimiento un efecto que se vincula a la belleza y acerca a la pureza. De ello la obra de Gupta, este oriental que no lo es tanto, está sobrada. Y su manera de entender un "orden imaginario de las cosas", desborda una catarata de imaginación singular y diferente, prosaica y poética, verdadera y global que, no sólo es legible, es creíble.

Everything is Inside, 2004
Taxi y bronce / Taxi and bronze
276 x 162 x 104 cm
Cortesía el artista / Courtesy the artist

"Me cautivan los objetos diminutos
ampliados hasta cuatro veces su tamaño"

SUBODH GUPTA

A veces lo único que nos convierte en lo que somos es todo aquello que nos rodea. Para mí, los grandes pensadores son la gente corriente y su vida diaria, sus prisas y sus asentamientos temporales. Y todo esto es lo que me inspira.

Crecí sin saber que acabaría siendo artista. En un hogar de clase trabajadora no te enseñaban a aspirar a nada más que a colmar las necesidades básicas. Sabía que quería hacer algo distinto, aunque no tenía ni idea de qué era. En casa había poca sensibilidad hacia la literatura y los escritores clásicos, y crecí en un ambiente de clase media, estrecho de miras, algo bastante habitual en la India.

Fui a la Escuela de Bellas Artes de Patna, otra pequeña tragedia, donde lo que se podía enseñar en cinco años se alargaba a casi siete, y sin mención alguna de la historia del arte ni de la vida y la obra de los grandes artistas. Un carpintero normal y corriente en occidente seguramente sabía más cosas que nosotros. ¡Una auténtica pena!

Apenas conocía a nadie y nunca me dejaron ser consciente de lo que nos depararía el arte a nosotros, los estudiantes, que un buen día nos veríamos arrojados al intenso dolor de un mundo desbordante, en constante expansión. Van Gogh, Picasso… eran los pocos nombres que conocíamos y sabíamos pronunciar.

Crecer en ese contexto fue un enorme reto en sí mismo, aunque nunca me faltó la motivación ni una mochila cargada de sueños. ¿Pero tenía suficiente con eso? Yo quería ser un pintor reconocido. Pronto mis compañeros de clase, que dibujaban y pintaban mejor que yo, se convirtieron en mi modelo a seguir. Imité sus técnicas artísticas y fueron mis profesores.

Me acuerdo de que, cuando tenía hambre, iba a buscar comida a los sitios más baratos. A veces recorría largas calles solitarias, en busca de esos *dhabas*, y un día caí bajo el hechizo de los carteles publicitarios. Me atraían y me cautivaban.

Los miraba, aún hambriento, intentando entender su lenguaje. Proseguí con mis estudios, pero supe que esa experiencia –la experiencia de haberme quedado atrapado por esas irresistibles imágenes grabadas en mi cabeza– sería el principio de mi viaje hacia el estudio del arte.

Me comunico a través de los objetos de deseo porque soy consciente de que me obsesionan. Sentí algo así en mi primer viaje a Europa. No importaba que me cachearan una y otra vez, cuando me soltaban, me quedaba siempre con los ojos abiertos, pasmado, y me dejaba llevar por el placer de observar.

Untitled, 2008
Acero inoxidable / Stainless steel
500 x 270 ø cm
Vista / Installation view *Art in the City*, Zúrich, Suiza / Zurich, Switzerland, 2012
Cortesía el artista y Hauser & Wirth / Courtesy the artist and Hauser & Wirth

Los carteles publicitarios son la luz que alumbra mi trayecto, y a veces aún los observo con alivio, sabiendo que mi viaje está iluminado por esos grandes carteles al acecho que guían mi camino.

¿Qué era ese apetito que sentía cada vez que iba a buscar un *dhaba* y me quedaba de pie bajo esos carteles resplandecientes y chillones de los que colgaba el anzuelo que te vendía una casita en Bihar? ¿Qué estaba buscando? Lo que me cautivaba eran esas imágenes descomunales, llamativas y brillantes, inmensas, pequeños objetos ampliados tres o cuatro veces su tamaño, para captar mejor tu atención. Mi arte es así. Ejemplifica la iconografía de una cotidianidad banal, precaria, provocadora y desbordante, de dimensiones gigantescas, totalmente desproporcionada, desprovista de su piel original para quedarse en simple masa y volumen.

Posteriormente, de nuevo en Europa, me quedé boquiabierto, sin palabras, al ver las obras de algunos maestros contemporáneos. Me contemplaban como carteles publicitarios, inmensos, que me atraían y me tentaban con sus gestos seductores. Me dejaron impresionado y a su lado me sentí diminuto.

Para mí, en eso consiste la grandeza del arte, en la capacidad de producir un excitante espectáculo catastrófico. A mí me ha cambiado la vida para siempre, aunque sigo fascinado por la vida sencilla que he vivido. La cocina, las salas de oración, los utensilios de acero inoxidable, los carteles publicitarios y los anuncios. Mi vida de pueblo se vio obligada a cambiar para siempre.

Subodh Gupta *The imaginary order of things*, CAC Málaga, 2013

Pure, 1999

Two Cows, 2003-2008

34   **All things are inside**, 2007

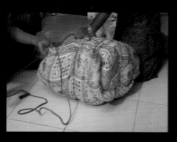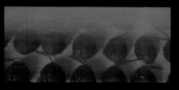

35

36   **Untitled**, 2008

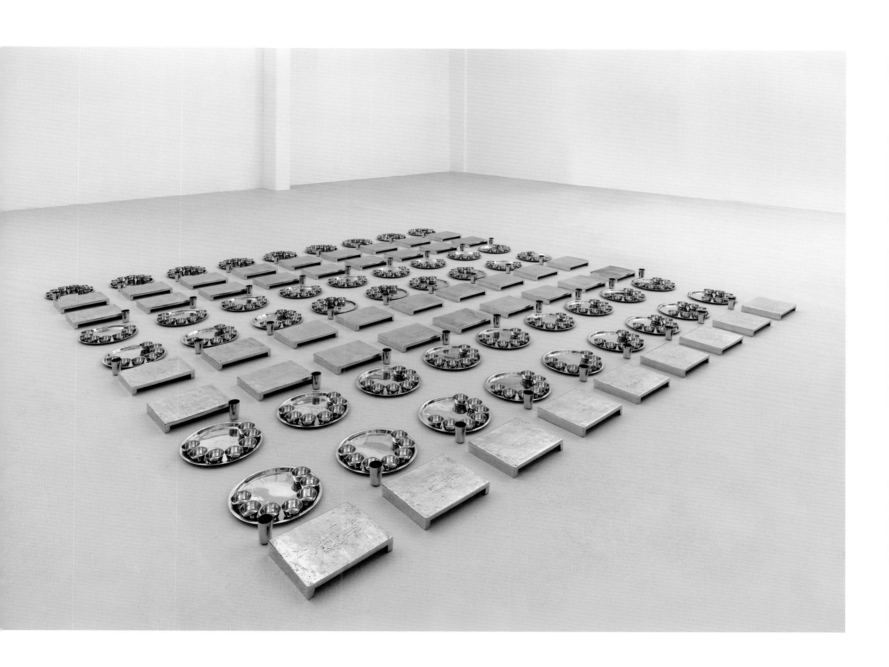

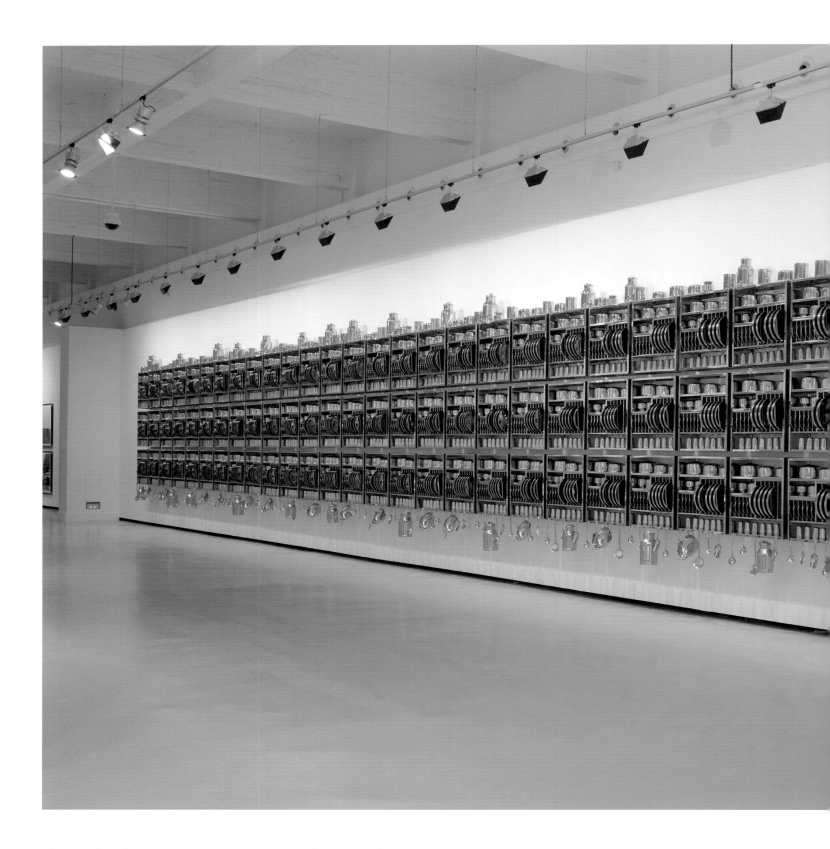

44   **Take off your shoes and wash your hands**, 2008

Atta, 2010

50   **Oil on canvas**, 2010

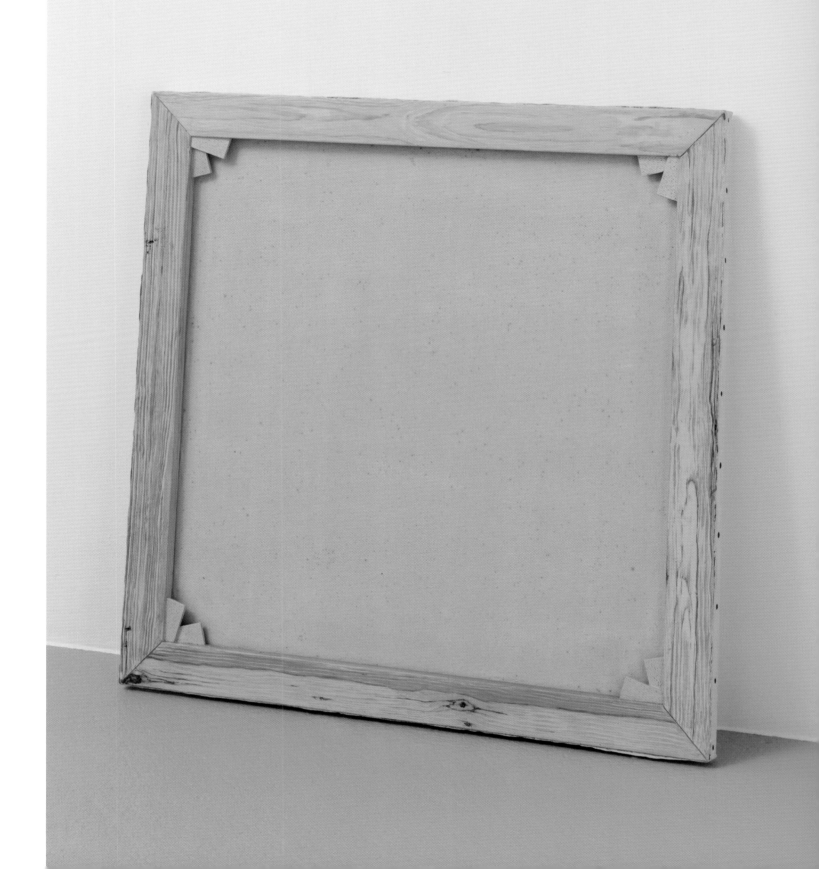

54   **A glass of water**, 2011

Pearl, 2011

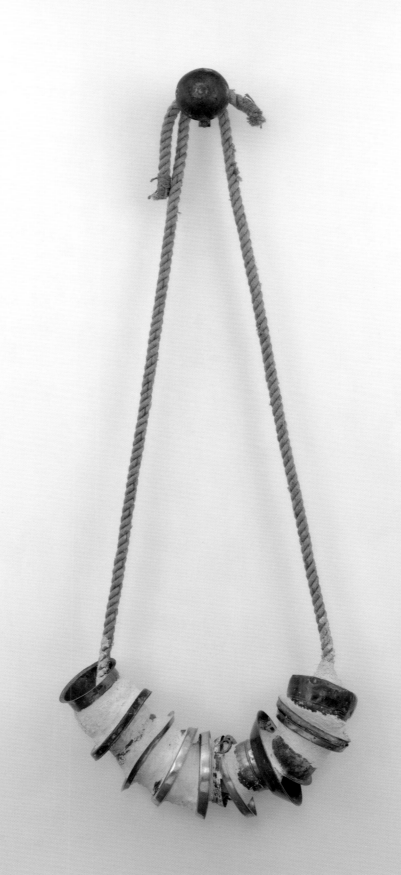

In this vessel lie groves and gardens, 2011

Family Nest No. 3, 2012

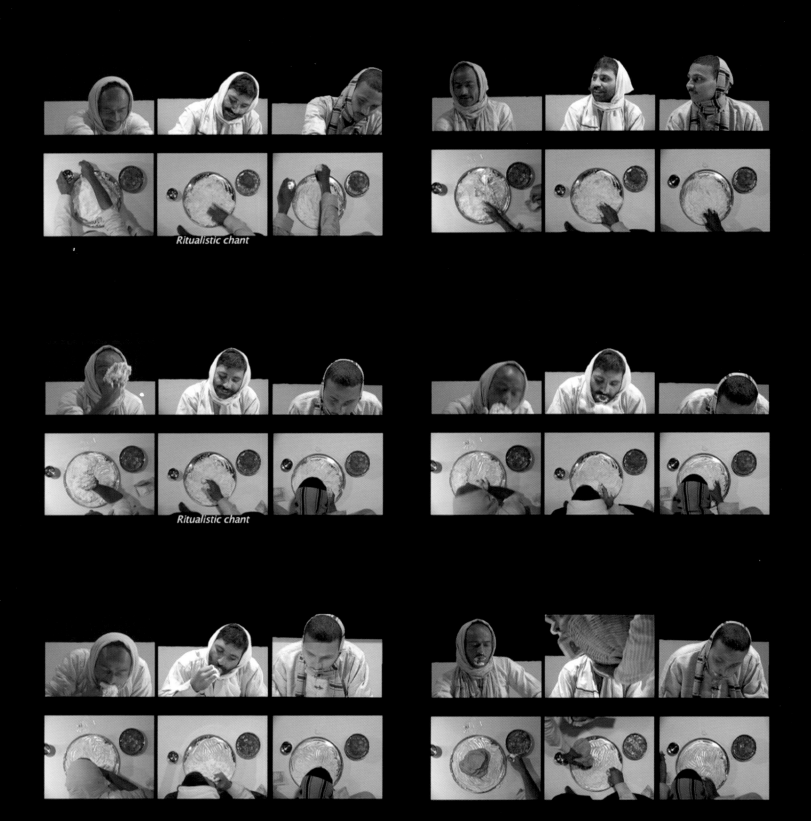

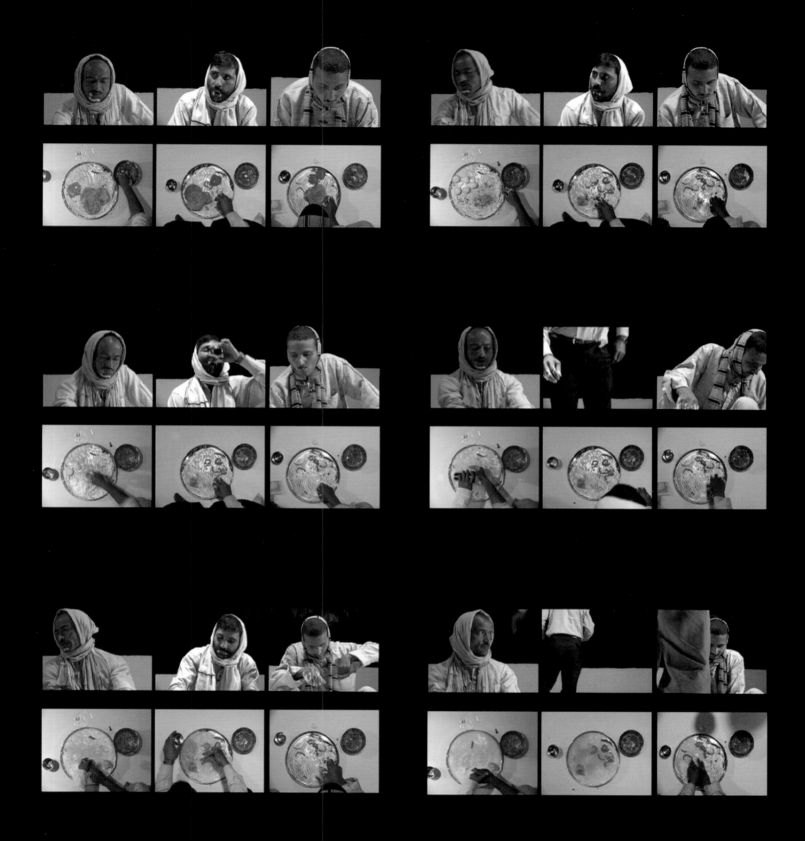

Subodh Gupta *The imaginary order of things*, CAC Málaga, 2013

Ancestor Cupboard, 2012

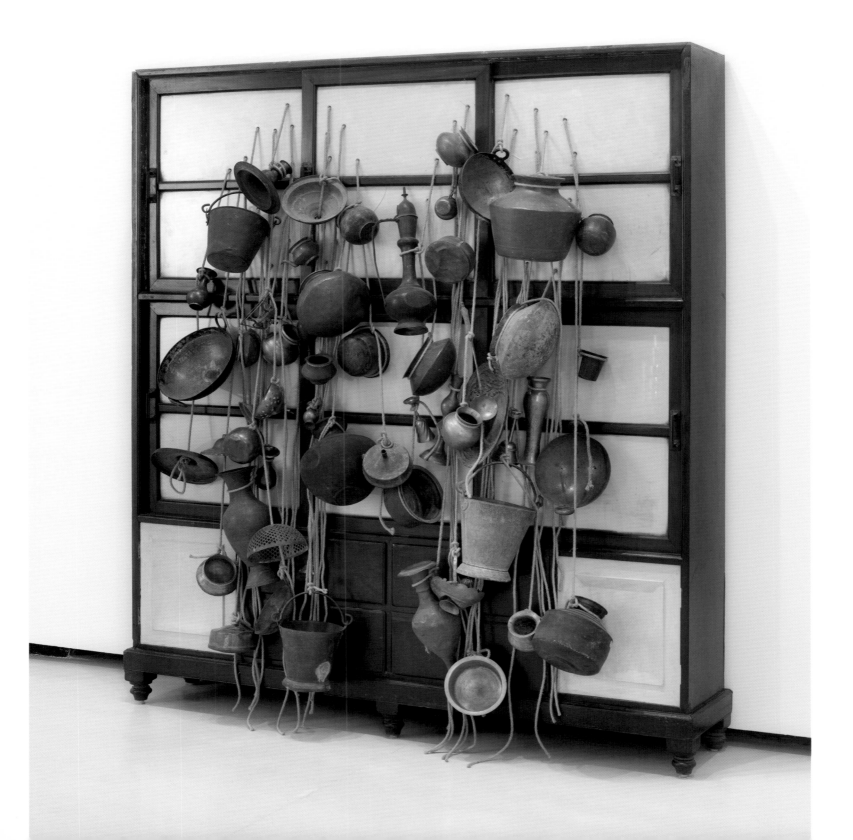

Cosmic Jewel, 2012

216 Sacks, 2012

Renunciation, 2012

All in the same boat, 2012-2013

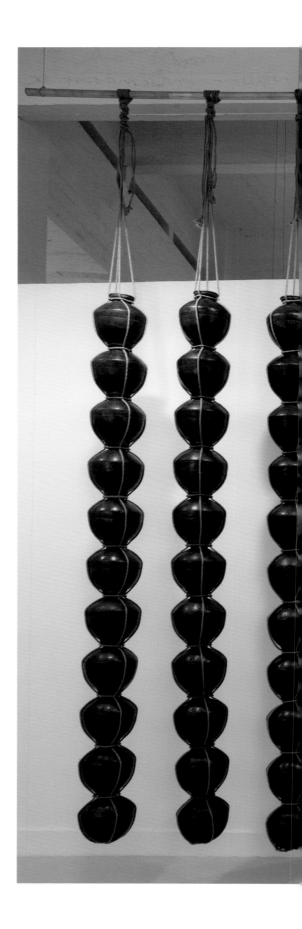

The imaginary order of things, 2012-2013

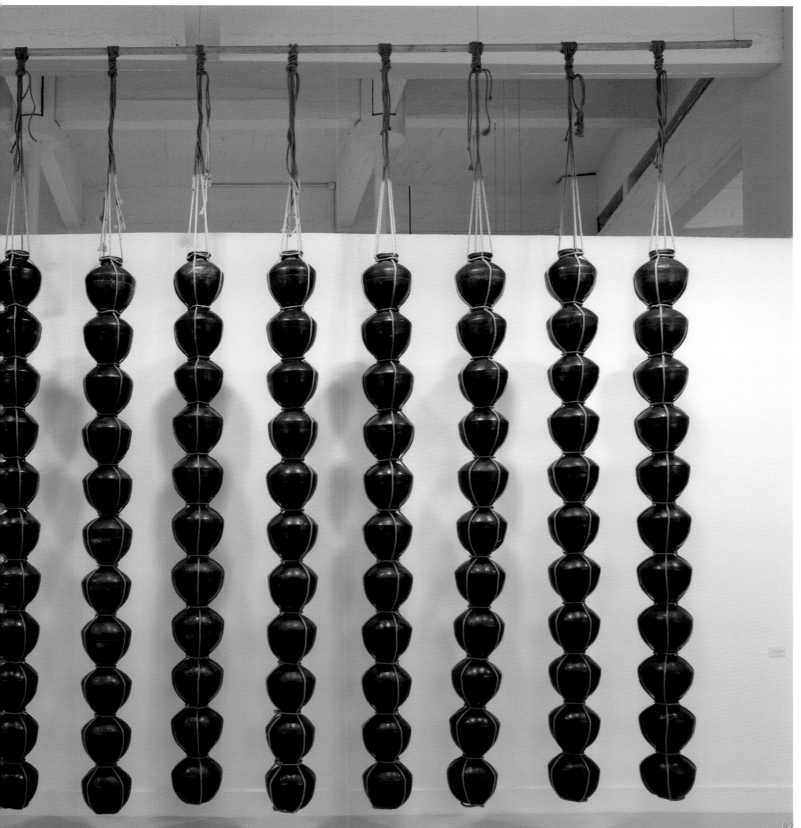

Season, 2013

Subodh Gupta *The imaginary order of things*, CAC Málaga, 2013

Subodh Gupta *The imaginary order of things*, CAC Málaga, 2013

Lista de obras | List of works

pp. 60-63
In this vessel lie groves and gardens, 2011
[En esta vasija hay árboles y jardines]
Tinaja de terracota, pintura, yute, luces, alambre, utensilios
de acero inoxidable y base de cemento con acero /
Terracotta jar, house paint, jute, light, wire, stainless steel
utensils, cement pedestal with steel
225 x 75 x 75,5 cm
Foto / Photo: José Luis Gutiérrez

pp. 64-65
Family Nest No. 3, 2012
[Nido de familia nº 3]
Mueble de cocina de acero inoxidable, utensilios de
cocina de acero inoxidable, utensilios viejos encontrados
de aluminio y latón, utensilios de acero esmaltados y
madera / Stainless steel cabinet, stainless steel utensils,
found old aluminium and brass utensils, enamel coated
steel utensils, wood
173 x 140 x 67 cm
Foto / Photo: Stefan Altenburger Photography Zürich

pp. 66-67
Spirit Eaters, 2012 *
[Personas que comen espíritus]
DVD
17:32 min

pp. 70-71
Ancestor Cupboard, 2012
[Alacena de antepasado]
Mueble de cocina de madera, utensilios viejos encontrados,
yeso de París, cuerda de yute y fibra de vidrio /
Wooden cabinet, found old utensils, plaster of Paris,
jute robe, fibreglass
144 x 218 x 71 cm
Foto / Photo: José Luis Gutiérrez

pp. 72-73
Cosmic Jewel, 2012
[Joya cósmica]
19 ollas de latón, cuerda y estructura de acero /
19 brass pots, rope, steel structure
301 x 235 x 105 cm
Foto / Photo: José Luis Gutiérrez

pp. 74-75
216 Sacks, 2012
[216 sacos]
Sacos de estopa / Hessian bags
Dimensiones variables / Variable dimensions
Foto / Photo: José Luis Gutiérrez

pp. 76-79
Renunciation, 2012
[Renuncia]
Técnica mixta / Mixed media
322 x 654 x 360 cm
Foto / Photo: José Luis Gutiérrez; Dominique Uldry

pp. 80-85
All in the same boat, 2012-2013
[Todos estamos en el mismo barco]
Técnica mixta / Mixed media
140 x 244 x 1161 cm
Foto / Photo: José Luis Gutiérrez

pp. 86-89
The imaginary order of things, 2012-2013
[El orden imaginario de las cosas]
Vasijas de latón y cuerda de yute / Brass pots, jute rope
Dimensiones variables / Variable dimensions
Foto / Photo: José Luis Gutiérrez

pp. 90-94
Season, 2013
[Estación]
Mangos de bronce pintados y máquina de coser /
Painted bronze mangoes, sewing table
98 x 111 x 40,5 cm
Foto / Photo: José Luis Gutiérrez; Dominique Uldry

* Obras no expuestas / Works not exhibited

Todas las obras si no indica lo contrario / All the works
otherwise stated: cortesía el artista y Hauser & Wirth /
courtesy the artist and Hauser & Wirth

Subodh Gupta

1964, Khagaul, Bihar, la India

Estudió Pintura en el College of Arts & Crafts, Patna, la India, 1983-88

Vive y trabaja en Nueva Delhi, la India, desde 1990

2013
Chevalier dans l'Ordre des Arts et des Lettres

2004
Residencia del gobierno francés en París

Profesor invitado en la L'École des Beaux-Arts, Francia

1997
Emerging Artist Award, Bose Pacia Modern, Nueva York, NY, EE. UU.

UNESCO-ASHBERG Bursaries for Artists, Gasworks Studio, Londres, Reino Unido

1996
All India Painting Exhibition, primer premio de M.F. Husain, Vadehra Art Gallery, Nueva Delhi, la India

1990-1991
Research Grant Scholarship, Lalit Kala Academy, Nueva Delhi, la India

1989
All India Festival, Dhanbad, la India

1987-1988
Students grant scholarship, Govt. of Bihar, Patna, la India

1987
State Level Art Exhibition of Bihar, la India

1986
All India Youth Festival, Madrás, la India

2013
Subodh Gupta. The imaginary order of things, CAC Málaga, Centro de Arte Contemporáneo, Málaga, España

What does the vessel contain, that the river does not, Hauser & Wirth, Londres, Reino Unido

Spirit Eaters, Kunstmuseum Thun, Thun, Suiza

2012
Line of Control, Kiran Nadar Museum, Nueva Delhi, la India

2011
Subodh Gupta, Sara Hildén Art Museum, Tampere, Finlandia

A glass of water, Hauser & Wirth, Nueva York, NY, EE. UU.

Subodh Gupta, Hauser & Wirth Outdoor Sculpture Southwood Garden, St. James's Church, Londres, Reino Unido

2010
Hauser & Wirth, Zúrich, Suiza

Et tu, Duchamp?, KÖR am Kunsthalle Wien project space Karlsplatz, Viena, Austria

Arario Gallery, Cheonan, Corea del Sur

Arario Gallery, Seúl, Corea del Sur

Faith matters, Pinchuk Art Centre, Kiev, Ucrania

Take off your shoes and wash your hands, Tramway, Glasgow, Reino Unido

Oil on canvas, Nature Morte, Nueva Delhi, la India

School, Hauser & Wirth, Londres, Reino Unido

2009
Common Man, Hauser & Wirth, Londres, Reino Unido

2008

Still Steal Steel, Jack Shainman Gallery, Nueva York, NY, EE. UU.

There is always Cinema, Galleria Continua, San Gimignano, Italia

Line of Control, Arario Beijing, Pekín, China

2007

Idol Thief, In SITU - Fabienne Leclerc, París, Francia

Start.Stop, Bodhi Art, Mumbai, la India

Silk Route, The Baltic, Gateshead, Reino Unido

2006

Hungry Gods, Nature Morte, Nueva Delhi, la India

Artes Mundi Prize, Cardiff National Museum, Cardiff, Reino Unido

2005

Jootha, In Situ - Fabienne Leclerc, París, Francia

I Go Home Every Single Day, Jack Shainman Gallery, Nueva York, NY, EE. UU.

Jootha, Sakshi Gallery, Mumbai, la India

2004

I Go Home Every Single Day, The Showroom Gallery, Londres, Reino Unido

2003

Saat Samunder Paar, Nature Morte, Nueva Delhi, la India

This Side is the Other Side, Art & Public - Cabinet PH, Ginebra, Suiza

2000

Recent Works, Nature Morte at Lokayata, Nueva Delhi, la India

1999

Recent Works, Gallery Foundation for Indian Arts, Ámsterdam, Países Bajos

1997

Bose Pacia Modern, Nueva York, NY, EE. UU.

The Way Home, Gallery Chemould, Mumbai, la India

Gasworks Gallery (con I Jayachandran), Londres, Reino Unido

1996

Grey Zones, Jehangir Art Gallery, Mumbai, la India

1995

Grey Zones, Academy of Fine Arts and Literature, Nueva Delhi, la India

1993

Recent Paintings, Gallery Espace, Nueva Delhi, la India

1990

Jamshedpur Tata Steel, Chitrakoot Art Gallery, Belidh Club, Kolkata, la India

1989

Recent Paintings, Shridhani Art Gallery, Nueva Delhi, la India

1986

Recent Paintings, Gandhi Sangharalya, Patna, la India

Exposiciones colectivas / Group Exhibitions

2013

Adventures of Truth, Fondation Maeght, Saint-Paul de Vence, Francia

2012

Food, Museé Ariana, Ginebra, Suiza

Kochi - Muziris Biennale 2012, Kochi, la India

Art, Talks and Sensations: The Island / A Game of Life, Manarat Al Saadiyat, Saadiyat Island, Abu Dhabi, Emiratos Árabes Unidos

Jing'An International Sculpture Project Biennial, Shanghai, China

Art in the City, Zúrich, Suiza

Ashes and Gold. A World's Journey, Museum Schloss Moyland, Bedburg-Hau, Alemania (itinerante)

India: Art Now, Arken Museum of Modern Art, Arken, Dinamarca

Massive / Intensive: Contemporary Art from India, Tel Aviv Museum of Art, Tel Aviv, Israel

Ashes and Gold. A World's Journey, MARTa Herford, Herford, Alemania (itinerante)

In Praise of Doubt, Punta della Dogana, François Pinault Foundation, Venecia, Italia

2011

Beijing Online Inlive. 10 Hands 100 Fingers, Galleria Continua, Pekín, China

Camulodunum, Colchester, Firstsite, Reino Unido

One, Another, FLAG Art Foundation, Nueva York, NY, EE. UU.

Home Spun, Devi Art Foundation, Nueva Delhi, la India

Artzuid 2011, Avenues of Berlage's Plan-Zuid, Ámsterdam, Países Bajos

Indian Highway V, MAXXI Museo Nazionale delle Arti del XXI Secolo, Roma, Italia (itinerante)

L'art del menjar. De la natura morta a Ferran Adrià, La Pedrera, Catalunya Caixa, Barcelona, España

In Praise of Doubt, Punta della Dogana, François Pinault Foundation, Venecia, Italia

París - Delhi - Bombay, Centre Pompidou, París, Francia

Indian Highway IV, Lyon Museum of Contemporary Art, Lyon, Francia (itinerante)

Time Unfolded, Kiran Nadar Museum of Art, Nueva Delhi, la India

2010

Indian Highway, Reykjavik Art Museum, Reikiavik, Islandia (itinerante)

Hareng Sauer: Ensor and Contemporary Art, S.M.A.K. - Stedelijk Museum voor Actuele Kunst, Gante, Bélgica

La Route de la Soie / The Silk Road, Tri Postal, Lille, Francia

REM(A)INDERS, Galleria Continua, Pekín, China

Urban Manners 2, SESC Pompeia, Sao Paulo, Brasil

Da Sopra, Castello Svevo di Bari, Bari, Italia

C'est la Vie. Vanities from Caravaggio to Damien Hirst, Fondation Dina Vierny - Musée Maillol, París, Francia

Indian Highway, Herning Kunstmuseum, Herning, Dinamarca (itinerante)

The Empire Strikes Back: Indian Art Today, The Saatchi Gallery, Londres, Reino Unido

Contemplating the Void, Guggenheim Museum, Nueva York, NY, EE. UU.

Art for the World (The Expo), Expo Shanghai 2010, Shanghai, China

Artefici contemporanei e difformità barocche, ARCOS, Museo d'Arte Contemporanea Sannio, Benevento, Italia

Monumental, Walsh Gallery, Chicago, IL, EE. UU.

2009

2009 Asian Art Biennial "Viewpoints and viewing points", National Taiwan Museum of Fine Arts, Taichung, Taiwán

The 6th Asia Pacific Triennial of Contemporary Art, Queensland Art Gallery, Brisbane, Australia

Altermodern: Tate Triennial 2009, Tate Britain, Londres, Reino Unido

Un Certain État du Monde? Works from the Pinault Collection, The Garage Centre for Contemporary Culture in Moscow, Moscú, Rusia

Narrativas de la India en el siglo XXI: entre la memoria y la historia, Casa Asia, Madrid, España

Passage to India Part II, Initial Access, Wolverhampton, Reino Unido

Who's Afraid of the Artists? A Selection of Works from the Pinault Collection, Palais des Arts de Dinard, Francia

Re-imagining Asia. A Thousand Years of Separation, The New Art Gallery Walsall, Walsall, Reino Unido (itinirante)

The 4th Fukuoka Asian Art Triennial, Fukuoka Asian Art Museum, Fukuoka, Japón

Chalo! India: A new Era of Indian Art, Essl Museum, Klosterneuburg, Austria; National Museum of Contemporary Art, Seúl, Corea del Sur (itinerante)

Indian Highway, Astrup Fearnley Museum, Oslo, Noruega (itinerante)

2008

Lustwarande 08 - Wanderland. 3rd Edition Lustwarande, Park de Oude Warande & Museum De Pont, Tilburg, Países Bajos

God & Goods - Spirituality and Mass Confusion, Villa Manin, Udine, Italia

Re-imagining Asia. A Thousand Years of Separation, Haus der Kulturen der Welt, Berlín, Alemania (itinerante)

Passage to India, Frank Cohen Collection at Initial Access, Wolverhampton, Reino Unido

CHANEL Mobile Art, Hong Kong, China; Tokio, Japón; Nueva York, NY, EE. UU. (itinerante)

Nueva Delhi - New Wave, Primo Marella Gallery, Milán, Italia

Frontlines: Notations from the Contemporary Indian Urban, Bodhi Art, Berlín, Alemania

Stadthimmel, Klaus Littman's project, Basilea, Suiza

Indian Focus. Artistes Indiens Contemporains dans la Collection de Claude Berri, Espace Claude Berri, París, Francia

Chalo! India: A new Era of Indian Art'Mori Art Museum, Tokio, Japón (itinerante)

Expanding Horizons, Bodhi Art, Mumbai, la India (itinerante)

Distant Nearness, The Nerman Museum of Contemporary Art at Johnson County Community College, Kansas City, KS, EE. UU.

Indian Highway, Serpentine Gallery, Londres, Reino Unido (itinerante)

Aurum. Gold in der zeitgenössischen Kunst, Centre PasquArt, Biel, Suiza

Martian Museum of Terrestrial Art, Barbican Art Gallery, Londres, Reino Unido

Everywhere is War (and Rumours of War), Bodhi Art, Mumbai, la India

Art Focus Jerusalem # 5, Jerusalén, Israel

Sphères 2008. Galleria Continua, Chantal Crousel, Hauser & Wirth, Galerie Krinzinger, Kamel Mennour, Galleria Continua / Le Moulin, Boissy-le-Châtel, Francia

Where in the World, Devi Art Foundation, Nueva Delhi, la India

Heavy Metal. On the Inexplicable Lightness of a Material, Kunsthalle zu Kiel, Kiel, Alemania

48º C Public. Art. Ecology, Nueva Delhi, la India

Second Lives: Remixing the Ordinary, Museum of Arts and Design, Nueva York, NY, EE. UU.

India Moderna, IVAM, Institut Valencia d'Art Modern, Valencia, España

New Narratives: Contemporary Art from India, Zimmerli Art Museum, Rutgers University, New Brunswick, NJ, EE. UU. (itinerante)

New Narratives: Contemporary Art from India, Salina Art Center, Salina, EE. UU. (itinerante)

2007

Urban Manners - 15 Contemporary Artists from India, Hangar Bicocca, Milán, Italia

Hungry God, Art Gallery of Ontario, Toronto, Canadá

India: Public Places / Private Spaces, The Newark Museum, Newark, NJ, EE. UU.

Nueva Delhi - New Wave, Primo Marella Gallery, Milán, Italia

La Gastronomie dans l'Art: De la Peinture Flamande à Andy Warhol, Artcurial, París, Francia

Dans ces Eaux là, Patrimoine et Creation Contemporaine au Château d'Avignon, Domaine du Château d'Avignon, Conseil général des Bouches-du-Rhone, Aviñón, Francia

New Narratives: Contemporary Art from India, The Chicago Department of Cultural Affairs Chicago, IL, EE. UU. (itinerante)

The Rusholme Project, Shisha, Manchester International Festival, Manchester, Reino Unido

Objects: Making / Unmaking, Vadehra Art Gallery, Nueva Delhi, la India

L' Emprise du lieu - L'experience Pommery #4, Reims, Francia

Private / Corporate IV, Sammlung Daimler Chrysler - Lekha and Anupam Poddar Collections, Berlín, Alemania

Sequence 1. Painting & Sculpture from the François Pinault Collection, Palazzo Grassi Venecia, Italia

Transitional Objects: Contemporary Still Life, Neuberger Museum of Art. Purchase College, State University of Nueva York, Purchase, NY, EE. UU.

Edge Of Desire: Recent Art in India, National Gallery of Modern Art, Mumbai, la India (itinerante)

2006
Altered, Stiched & Gathered, P.S.1 MoMA, Nueva York, NY, EE. UU.

Taipei Biennial 2006, Taipéi, Taiwán

Venice - Istanbul, Istanbul Modern, Estambul, Turquía

Contemporary India, Palais des Beaux-Arts de Bruxelles, Bruselas, Bélgica

Balance and Power, Rose Art Museum, Waltham, MA, EE. UU.

Transitional Objects: Contemporary Still Life, Neuberger Museum of Art, Nueva York, NY, EE. UU.

Edge Of Desire: Recent Art in India, Montalvo Arts Center, Saratoga CA, EE. UU.; Berkeley Arts Museum, Berkeley, CA, EE. UU. (itinerante)

Nuit Blanche, Eglise Saint Bernard et vitrine de la Galerie in Situ, París, Francia

Bombaysers de Lille, Lille 3000, Lille, Francia

Hungry Gods, Arario Gallery, Pekín, China

Bronze, Gallery Espace, Nueva Delhi, la India

Made by Indians. Art on the Beach #5, Galerie Enrico Navarra, Plage de Pampelonne, Commune de Ramatuelle, Francia

If it Didn't Exist You'd Have to Invent it, The Showroom Gallery, Londres, Reino Unido

L' Inde dans tous les Sens, Louis Vuitton Showroom, París, Francia

Edge Of Desire: Recent Art in India, MARCO - Museo de Arte Contemporáneo, Monterrey, Mexico (itinerante)

2005
Balance and Power: Performance and Surveillance in Video Art, Krannert Art Museum, Champaign, IL, EE. UU.

Always a little Further, La Biennale di Venezia, Venecia, Italia

Universal Experience: Art, Life and the Tourist's Eye, Museum of Contemporary Art, Chicago, IL, EE. UU.; Hayward Gallery, Londres, Reino Unido (itinerante)

Weightless Space, The Herzliya Museum Of Contemporary Art, Herzliya, Israel

Dialectics of Hope, The Moscow Biennale of Contemporary Art, Moscú, Rusia

Mom and Pop, Walsh Gallery, Chicago, IL, EE. UU.

Indian Summer, École Nationale Supérieure des Beaux Arts, París, Francia

Edge Of Desire: Recent Art in India, Queens Museum of Modern Art, Queens, NY, EE. UU.; The Asia Society, Nueva York, NY, EE. UU.; Museo Tamayo, Ciudad de México, México (itinerante)

2004

Indian Video Art: History in Motion, Fukuoka Asian Art Museum, Fukuoka, Japón

Two-Man Show, Centre A - Vancouver International Centre for Contemporary Art, Vancouver, Canadá

Another Passage to India, Saisons Indiennes à Genève, Ginebra, Suiza

Vanitas Vanitatum, Sakshi Gallery, Mumbai, la India

Drawings, The Eagle Gallery, Londres, Reino Unido

The SNEEZE, a Featured Film by 80 artists x 80 seconds 106 minutes, Gazon Rouge Gallery, Atenas, Grecia

Postkort fra Cuba, Henie Onstad Kunstsenter, Høvikodden, Noruega

Edge Of Desire: Recent Art in India, The Art Gallery of Western Australia, Perth, Australia (itinerante)

2003

8. Biennale Havanna, La Habana, Cuba

Crossing Generations: diVERGE, Gallery Chemould, Mumbai, la India

Body. City. Citing Contemporary Culture in India, House of World Cultures, Berlín, Alemania

An Apparent Calm which is in Fact a Perfectly Balanced Tension, Grantpirrie Gallery, Sídney, Australia

HEAT, Bose Pacia Modern, Nueva York, NY, EE. UU.

The Tree from the Seed, Contemporary Art from India, Henie Onstad Kunstsenter, Høvikodden, Noruega

Bad Taste, Apparao Galleries, Apeejay New Media Centre, Nueva Delhi, la India

2002

Under Construction, Japan Foundation y Tokyo Opera City Art Gallery, Japón

Private Mythologies of the Personal and the Political, Apeejay Media Gallery, Faridabad, la India

Creative Space, Sakshi Gallery at Habitat Centre, Nueva Delhi, la India

Multi Media Art Asia Pacific, Pekín, China

Busan Biennale, Busan Metropolitan Art Museum, Busan, Corea del Sur

Self: Contemporary Indian Video Art, IMA - Institute of Modern Art, Brisbane, Australia

Indian Art: Home-Street-Shrine-Bazaar-Museum, Manchester City Art Gallery, Manchester, Reino Unido

Cinema Stills, Apparao Galleries, India Habitat Centre, Nueva Delhi, la India

Kapital & Karma, Kunsthalle Wien, Viena, Austria

Sorry for the Inconvenience, Project 304, Bangkok, Thailandia

Inaugural Show, Palais de Tokyo, París, Francia

Sidewinder, CIMA Gallery, Kolkata, la India; India Habitat Centre, Nueva Delhi, la India; Coomarswamy Hall, The Prince of Wales Museum of Western India, Mumbai, la India (Itinerante)

Photosphere, Nature Morte, Nueva Delhi, la India

2001

Post Residency Show, National Gallery Of Modern Art, Mumbai, la India

Bollywood has arrived, Passenger Terminal, Ámsterdam, Países Bajos

Post Production (Sampling, Programming & Displaying), Galleria Continua, San Gimignano, Italia

Context as Content - Museum as Metaphor - Museum of Fine Art, Museum of Fine Art, Chandigarh, la India; Nature Morte, Nueva Delhi, la India (itinerante)

2000

Vilas, Birla Academy, Mumbai, la India

I love Video Art, Theatre de Strasbourg et le Forum itinerant, Estrasburgo, Francia

Print et.com, Max Muller Bhawan, Nueva Delhi, la India

Invisible Boundary: Metamorphosed Asian Art, Asian Section of the Kwangju Biennale 2000, Gwangju, Corea del Sur; Niigata City Prefectural Civil Centre Gallery, Niigata, Japón; Utsunomiya Museum of Art, Utsunomiya, Japón (itinerante)

Negotiations, CRAC Alsace - Centre Rhénan d'Art Contemporain, Sète, Francia

1999

The First Fukuoka Asian Art Triennale, Fukuoka Asian Art Museum, Fukuoka, Japón

Of based on, or obtained, Nature Morte, Nueva Delhi, la India

Impact, Jim Beard Gallery at CCA, Nueva Delhi, la India

Indian Artists, Nature Morte, Sídney, Australia

Edge of Century, Art India, Nueva Delhi, la India

1998

New Millenium, New Media, Jehangir Art Gallery, Mumbai, la India

Kendal Wallah- Through Indian Eyes, Brewery Arts Centre, Kendal, Reino Unido

1997

UNESCO-ASHBERG Bursaries for Artists hosted by InIVA, Gasworks Studios, Londres, Reino Unido

Khoj International Artists Exhibition, British Council, Nueva Delhi, la India

Points of Contact, Shirley Fiterman Gallery, Nueva York, NY, EE. UU.

1996

Indo-Austrian Artists' Workshop, Sanskriti Kendra, Nueva Delhi, la India

Indo-Cuban Exhibition of Contemporary Art, Lalit Kala Academy, Nueva Delhi, la India

1995

Nessuno Tocchi Caino (Hands off Cain), La Biennale di Venezia, Venecia, Italia

1994

Young Generation from Bihar, Faculty of Fine Arts, M.S. University, Baroda, la India

Young Contemporary Artists, Birla Academy, Kolkata, la India

Drawings '94, Gallery Escape of AIFACS Gallery, Nueva Delhi, la India

1993

Contemporary Indian Artists, Gallery Escape, Dubai, Emiratos Árabes Unidos

1991

Husain Ki Sarai, Vadehra Art Gallery, Nueva Delhi, la India

Research Grant Scholars Exhibition, Lalit Kala Academy, Nueva Delhi, Lucknow, Madrás, la India

Imprints of our Time, Jehangir Art Gallery, Mumbai, la India

1990

All India Painting Exhibition, Vadehra Art Gallery, Rabindra Bhawan, Nueva Delhi, la India

1989

Contemporary Artists of Bihar, Rabindra Bhawan, Nueva Delhi, la India

1987

Young Painters of Bihar, Patna, la India

1983

Group of AB Exhibition, Patna, Bihar, la India

All India Drawing and Craft Exhibition, Patna, la India

Traducción | **Translation**

FRANCISCO DE LA TORRE PRADOS | Mayor of Málaga

Contemporary Art Centre of Málaga is presenting the exhibition *Subodh Gupta. The imaginary order of things*, the first solo exhibition of the work of this Indian artist in Spain. It comprises around nineteen works, sculptures, installations and video, some not previously exhibited.

One of Subodh Gupta's distinguishing characteristics is the way in which he conveys the culture of his country from a viewpoint that is completely different to the vision offered to us by the media or cinema. Utensils and everyday objects used by any Indian family are the basic material of his work, in addition to the use of a range of materials including wood, bronze and marble.

The union of tradition and modernity and the artist's interpretation of religion through the importance that he concedes to Indian foodstuffs and rituals are revealed in Subodh Gupta's work from a unique viewpoint, making use of a contemporary aesthetic that is far removed from any stereotype or cultural cliché.

Once again this exhibition at the CAC Málaga provides visitors with a unique opportunity to appreciate the work of one of the most important artists within the field of international contemporary art today. It is also another indication of the Centre's commitment to making Málaga a reference point for contemporary art from around the world.

Subodh Gupta, the poetic effect of objects and memory

FERNANDO FRANCÉS | Director of CAC Málaga

Since the appearance of Homo sapiens, who was capable of painting the cave of Altamira in the Magdalenian period, and even long before that, man has used creative processes in an attempt to explain aspects of the physical and the spiritual that were relevant to him in his attempt to explain his own existence, or which he did not understand, focusing on the search for truly imaginative answers to his doubts.

All these processes of exploration are characterised by the global nature of their interpretation. Art has the unique feature of being a language comprehensible to the gaze of most eyes, independent of the language that the viewer speaks, with the obvious limitations of that person's cultural level in conceptual terms. Even the art of representation or the hieroglyphic can be understood by individuals living thousands of years later.

In addition, art is capable of transmitting messages in the form of commitment or poetry, and both are easily accessible to a large number of people in a world as global as the present one. To achieve a high degree of interaction it may be necessary to grasp all the nuances and to be familiar with the details of the social context in which that art has been created, but in any case, and by making use of the viewer's free interpretation, art can succeed in transmitting sensations and messages that are comprehensible to all. My intention is not to state that art is communication, although it can also be in a collateral manner, but this is not its primary function or raison d'être. What I do consider essential, indeed inherent, is art's capacity to reflect on life, on the reality of human existence and the causes and consequences of our relationships and actions. I also sincerely believe that any art that does not develop that capacity becomes totally obsolete.

Art that arises from experience, from social, political, economic and cultural reality and from today's ongoing debates in a free, unprejudiced manner is the type that has more purity and conviction. At the same time, that extra content gives it much more authenticity and credibility. The opposite case would be art that only defines itself as beauty with an exclusively aesthetic intent. Art reinvents itself every day and contemporary art cannot stand aside from what is happening in the world and from interpreting the sociological, intellectual and even environmental processes that we are currently experiencing. The type of art that takes its starting point from the human condition clearly has a capacity for connection. The key lies in producing it in a different way, reinventing creative processes, introducing innovative viewpoints that contribute original ways of understanding what already seems to have been invented. In this quest for something different, the life experience of artists from different places and cultures, the biography of each one, is fundamental to achieving that end. The alternative would be an artist who took refuge in a glass bubble and remained unresponsive and insensitive to what happened outside it. The ivory towers that separate the artist from reality are becoming increasingly anachronistic and the art that emerges from them is losing the component of responsibility and commitment that is needed if it is to move us.

Paradoxically, over the years, the agents of art – principally curators and those responsible for museum programming – in what might be seen as a championing of corporatism, have influenced creative action, redirecting it and selecting only those actions that seem to be homogenous in conceptual terms and leaving out all other types of art that emerge from positions of independence and freedom. There are few artists who escape the control of critics and curators, who tend to share the viewpoint that art should not move us but should solely be the consequence of a type of political thinking or of a historical and intellectual process. However, it is clear that thinking and commitment without emotion ultimately end up orphaned and will almost undoubtedly be forgotten over the years.

What is clear is that, as time passes, it is increasingly difficult to find all these arguments for authenticity and truth in a single work of art or in a single artist. The world has become ever more trivialised and art has not been unaffected by that process. When visiting exhibitions and art fairs, looking for something that moves us, it is often frustrating when this does not happen and one gains the impression that many artists live and produce their work from the standpoint of their agents' parameters and criteria and from their own, personal idiosyncrasies, concealing their authentic, free thinking. I greatly miss a degree of freedom of expression of a type found in an academic context in universities. It may be for this reason, and while granting that the general cultural level of the population has gone up notably everywhere, contemporary art is now very remote from real people, who are reluctant to understand it even though such comprehension is quite possible.

Some years ago, when visiting yet another of the world's increasingly predictable and bland art fairs, I was captivated by an exquisite composition of shiny metal objects carefully arranged in a circle: plates and cutlery that floated in the air, suspended by fine nylon threads from the ceiling in precarious equilibrium. The draught created by people passing by the work made the pieces move slowly while even the air-conditioning disturbed the fragile stillness of these objects. My initial impression was the result of an aesthetic attraction that lasted for a few minutes. The work then started to speak in its attempt to attract attention for other reasons that would be missed by a rapid, initial gaze. Despite the fact that the setting was not the most appropriate for it, that most people passed by without paying attention to this small installation and despite its apparently modest nature, a depth-charge had gone off inside me, I'm not sure where: in my heart, brain or stomach, or perhaps in all of them at once.

I had of course seen other works by Subodh Gupta in the past on various occasions, for example, at the Palais de Tokyo and at the 51st Venice Biennial where he presented *Curry* of 2005, the forerunner to *Take off your shoes and wash your hands* of 2008, an installation now to be seen at the CAC Málaga. However, his work had never made such an impression on me. It is strange how these mental triggers function, the connections between the gaze and the brain. Or perhaps it is a question of predisposition, of intellectual connection, of coinciding with regard to a shared set of interests and concerns. What is true is that Gupta's work encouraged not only my interest in him but also in India. My relationship with the country had been confined up to that point to a series of articles that I wrote in my youth, when I was a conscientious objector, on Mahatma Gandhi and non-violence.

One of my ongoing and long-lasting interests in the art world has been that of seeking out artists whose work particularly moves me. When this occurs – as it has with artists as diverse as William Kentridge, Lawrence Weiner, Tracey Emin, Raymond Pettibon and Ai Weiwei – I am left with the certainty that art is undoubtedly one of the few medicines capable of healing the world's ills and at the same time calming inner torments, neutralising the monsters of the subconscious. I have had this experience in recent years with every work by Subodh Gupta that I have encountered and my fascination with his ideas, his work and his position as an artist has grown ceaselessly and systematically.

With Gupta there is an aspect that confers the highest degree of credibility on his work and which is consequently not particularly frequent as a statement of principles among other artists of his generation. I refer to his interest in reflecting on the close-at-hand. It is here that the young artist, at the start of his career, found the keys to inventing his own artistic terrain. Gupta has commented on the importance for him of his early installation of 29 stools that he created in the Sanskriti Kendra in Delhi where he lived with other artists. That work opened the way towards a fascinating world of images and memories of his childhood. As a result, his personal experience became his primary source of inspiration for his thinking and also contributed to making his work distinctive and different, something that Gupta has always sought out in an exercise that I consider essential in the present day and which can be related to the desire not to follow official criteria, forms and themes. Gupta rediscovered from his childhood the attraction that cooking held for him and his interest in kitchen equipment. The utensils and crockery used in the kitchen particularly fascinated him. Steel containers for storing food and for cooking were not only a sign of progress among India's emerging new middle class but also a symbol of the display of that progress. In addition, in comparison to wood or ceramic, metal represents major technological advances, as these vessels are more resistant and hygienic. The memory that the artist has of this period and his focus on cookery is not a distinguishing feature of India per se. I recall having the same feelings about my childhood in Spain in the 1960s. The kitchen marked out the rhythm of the day, with the metal utensils hanging from a bar in the kitchen, not just so that they were in easy reach but also as a sign of modernity, luxury and decoration. Similarly, when I see bicycles or mopeds with saucepans hanging from the handlebars or from the sides I remember how, as a child, I went from the beach house to the village for fresh milk every evening. I now know that something similar happened in Gupta's house in Bihar where he spent his childhood. It is interesting that it should be an Indian artist, from a far-off country and very different culture, who should help me to recall my own childhood and youth by remembering his own.

Over time the metal kitchen items have become not just the elements that constitute a complete and complex body of work, the pieces that complete the vision of a whole, but also the very primary material with which Subodh Gupta defines the symbolism, the material and the message. In the artist's work we encounter the co-existence of ongoing dichotomies that bring about the opposition between the two halves of his action and thinking. The result is a permanent dialogue between works which, based on memories and images of everyday life in any Indian city or village, consciously reflect a degree of disorder and chaos that conveys the viewer of the work from the most endemic part of popular Indian tradition (*Ancestor Cupboard*, 2012, 216 *Sacks*, 2012, *Season*, 2013, *Two Cows*, 2003-08, or even *All in the same boat*, 2012-13) to other areas characterised by order, balance, the methodical detachment of procedures characteristic of a post-industrial period and ones that suggest the influence of Minimalism (*School*, 2008, *Take off your shoes and wash your hands*, 2008, and *Faith Matters*, 2007-08).

Gupta explores the immediately obvious side of Indian life through his most recognisable and accessible iconographic repertoire in order to offer a profound investigation of the meanings of a vigorous and complex social evolution. Nonetheless, his work cannot in any sense be understood as a gesture of political commitment or as art resulting from political action, of the type so dear to post-modern curators. He limits himself to transcribing a concrete reality that he knows and has experienced at first hand into a universal language. The global nature of a certain type of art, constructed from the starting point of sentiment, means that his memories are comprehensible for a wide-range and diverse public, in the manner of a diary of emotions. This capacity to reach out is furthermore one of the artist's distinguishing features. Gupta set out in an almost obsessive manner to create a different type of art but at the same time that he succeeding in establishing his repertoire of ideas, he also managed to make the reading codes of its intentions different. It is precisely here that we find the most conceptual aspect of his creative process. Gupta lives and works in New Delhi, which gives credibility to his thinking and helps to ensure that his work is not remote from his daily life. As with Ai Weiwei in Beijing or Kentridge in Johannesburg, Gupta is one of the few artists who has not succumbed to the success of his work in the West and consequently abandoned the original concept of his art and thinking, which are so intimately connected to his place of residence. It is from New Delhi that Gupta builds up a compendium of ideas that refer to a message, which may be poetic or everyday, but which in both cases contributes to formulating a discourse on his own history and that of his country. As I have explained in this text, despite working at the very heart of Indian culture, in Gupta's oeuvre we find continual references to the history of modern Western art, not so much in formal terms but through a type of appropriationism used in the services of his own creative process. In works that aim at immersion in tradition through the use of old materials, be they kitchen implements, containers, musical instruments or a simple pyramid of sacks (*Cosmic Jewel*, 2012), the resulting appearance is that of a type of *povera* accumulation. In others, however, the emotion, if not the influence, is markedly minimalist (*Untitled*, 2008, or *Faith Matters*, 2007-08), or conceptual (*Oil on canvas*, 2010, or *A glass of water*, 2011), while on numerous occasions his work could even be seen as a ready-made (*216 Sacks*, 2012), given that he often finds the materials in his immediate surroundings. Whatever the case, whether re-codifying an object, reproducing it in steel or bronze, or using it in the state in which it has been found or purchased and creating a new reality from the idea of it, Gupta has succeeded in inventing a new way of writing an autobiography imbued with truth and emotion.

Subodh Gupta's work is certainly not devoid of cultural, religious and even geographical commitment. The installation *Renunciation* of 2012, based on a reproduction of the monumental Buddhas of Bamiyan in Afghanistan after they were destroyed by the Taliban, is a good example. Through small holes the viewer can see a group of relics of absence inside this sacred Buddhist mountain. Like the hermits of Meteora in Thessaly and elsewhere, Buddha renounced all worldly goods in order to live alone in meditation and to achieve the spiritual state in which he could free men from their suffering.

Here again we have one of the contrasts of dichotomies referred to earlier. While the metal objects with which Gupta's sculptures are crammed – trays, cook pots, saucepans, plates, cutlery, cups, dishes, pots, glasses, bowls and crockery – reveal not just the lifestyle but also the social ascent of the Indian middle-classes and their aspirations to achieve a more elevated social level, *Renunciation* represents one of the most deep-rooted concepts in Hinduism: the necessity to live with nothing in order to achieve a state of purity. We need to remember that Gupta does not practice any religion, as a result of which his commitment to it is that of an observer who has lived the experience but who relates to it with the distance of time. There is thus a certain emotional distance in the way of presenting his vision on the subject when it has a religious or political origin. His true goal and personal commitment is only with art, and once again in this regard he is characterised by a desire for commitment with a creative process that combines philosophy and process. While the war in Afghanistan has no relationship with this work, war, violence and the fact that India is one of the countries to have nuclear weapons appears in an extremely subtle way in his work (*Line of Control*, 2008, *Ghandi's Three Monkeys*, 2008, and *1 K.G. WAR*, 2007).

What mother has never said to her child – or at least to a child who does not play exclusively with video games or the computer – something like "Take your shoes off and wash your hands before you eat"? It would seem that childhood memories are the same the world over. There are significant doses of irony and humour in Gupta's artistic approach, to be found in many of his works and certainly in many of his titles. Among them are *Gandhi's Three Monkeys*, 2008, or *Family Nest No. 3*, 2012, in which a harmonious and compact group of similar objects is suddenly surrounded by others of different shapes, colours and origins, hanging on as best they can, suspended from the corners and located on the periphery of this original nucleus, which is in fact the way families grow in reality. In addition, the spirit that Gupta conveys in his daily life and way of being is also a warning to the viewer, something like: "Be careful! This is not something really serious." Perhaps this attitude of permanent controversy, ambiguity and contradiction also contributes to that game of seduction in which his work entrapped me so many years ago.

As a child, Gupta was not only fascinated by kitchen utensils but also with transport, specifically with the machines used for it. Bicycles (*Cow*, 2005, or *Two Cows*, 2003-08), tricycles (*Cheap Rice*, 2006), motorcycles (*Bullet*, 2006-07), cars (*Doot*, 2003) and boats (*What does the vessel contain, that the river does not*, 2012) constantly reappear in his work. In some cases these vehicles are weighed down with saucepans and cooking pots to evoke the activities of daily life in India: the importance of movement or of representation, given that Gupta has, for example, defined bicycles as the city's mechanised cows; the need to transport water, milk or oil; the symbol of social status or of the prosperity of the rich; status, represented by vehicles of all types and by cooking vessels that contain nothing but spirituality, often for the price of a few rupees. In contrast, we also find cars and carts filled with suitcases and bundles (*Everything is Inside*, 2004), in which the artist's concerns shift to the Indian population's continuous process of migration, either from India to abroad or from rural areas to the city. Migration is, however, not just a question of objects but of the spirit, the soul, thought and culture. This is too heavy a weight to leave behind almost everything during such migratory journeys, which are not just from one place to another on the planet but are also internal ones taking place inside people.

Subodh Gupta is possibly the most poetic artist in the world. He does not renounce the material, in fact, quite the opposite. By basing himself on it to the limits of exaggeration, monumentality and the baroque (*Bombaysers de Lille*, a homage to the victims of the 2004 tsunami), he succeeds in making emotion – a sentiment as close-at-hand as it is rare – spread into and overturn all the boundaries and walls of thinking and reason. He is a sort of modern Robin Hood who appropriates the Indian drama, re-codifies it, imbues it with an emotional charge and gives it back to us as a gift for the eyes and mind. Nothing is the result of chance in his work. The very process of thought is a ritual or ceremony in which, like a skilled alchemist, he revives memories of childhood and youth, symbols and pots and pans, as if they were objects of desire or cult objects or both at the same time. He gives them patinas that bear messages: the bronzes and golds of the sacred, the steel of industrial progress. The result is a sort of equilibrium between antiquity and the avant-garde, chaos and order, harmony and upheaval, emotion and suspense. Only the skill of a poet can harmonise all these elements in a work of art with the certainty that there are no untruths in his discourse. The power to convince that is characteristic of Gupta's work is only possible through his existential commitment to his work. One creates the other just as spirit and matter constitute man. It is particularly gratifying to appreciate this visionary artist's ability to bring values, rituals, customs and habits of the East to a Western sensibility and to do so from the starting point of emotion. Traditionally, in Western culture, from the Renaissance onwards the shiny, gleaming surface has been an effect associated with beauty and one close to purity. The work of Gupta – an oriental who is not exactly one – is filled with this effect, as is his way of understanding an "imaginary order of things", a great outpouring of unique and distinctive imagination, at once mundane and poetic, true and global, and one that is not just legible but also believable.

"I'm captivated by tiny objects grown to four times their size"

SUBODH GUPTA

There are times when there is nothing other than what is around us that makes us who we are. For me, the great thinkers are the common people, with their everyday existence; their hurried lives and makeshift settlements. You must see this as the place I look to be inspired.

I grew up not knowing that I would be an artist. Nobody in a working class household was taught to aspire beyond the daily rigour of bread and butter. I knew I wanted to do something different; what that was, I had no idea. In a house with little exposure to renowned authors or classic literature, all I ever had was an insular, middle-class life, which is not uncommon throughout India.

I went to the Patna College of Art and that was another minor tragedy. Where five years' worth of teaching is dragged on for almost seven years, with no mention of art history or great peer artists, their work and lives. An average carpenter in the West possibly ended up knowing more than we did. What a pity that was!

I hardly knew anyone and was never made aware of what the art world held for us students, who'd one day be thrown into the throes of a bustling, ever expanding realm. Van Gogh, Picasso... a few names we uttered and knew.

Growing up in this way was a massive challenge in itself. Undoubtedly, there was never a lack of motivation, and a bagful of dreams, but how could this ever be enough? I wanted to be a renowned painter. And my classmates who were drawing and painting better than me quickly became my role models. I followed their ways of art-making and they became my teachers.

I remember, when I was hungry, I looked for food at the cheapest places I could find. Walking down lonely roads, on the way to these dhabas I fell under the spell of billboards. I was attracted to them and arrested by them.

I'd look up, still hungry, trying to slowly understand their language. I continued my studies, but I knew that this experience – the experience of being transfixed by these irresistible images embedded on my horizon – was the beginning of my journey into the study of art.

I communicate using the objects of desire because I know enough to acknowledge that they haunt me. I felt something of this in Europe on my first trip there. Never mind that I was checked and crosschecked, every time I was let go, only to be left wide-eyed and astonished as one can be who is allowed to indulget in the pleasure of seeing.

Billboards litter the path of my journey, and even now, I look up every so often with relief, knowing that my journey is lit large by looming signs that guide my way.

What was that hunger I felt every time I was on my way to a dhaba and waited under these heavily lit, garish billboards dangling consumerist bait for a village in Bihar? What was it I was looking for? What captivated me were these roaring images, loud and bright, larger than life, tiny objects grown to three, four times their size, to grab our attention better. My art is thus. Exemplifying the iconography of a banal, precarious, edgy and bustling everyday life humongous in magnitude, blown out of proportions, peeled from their ordinary skin by their sheer mass and volume.

Later, again in Europe, I was thrilled beyond words to stand in front of the works of some contemporary masters. These looked to me like billboards, larger than life, beckoning me, tempting me with their inviting gestures. I felt in awe of them and I felt dwarfed in comparison.

For me, this is what great art is capable of producing – a delicious catastrophe of spectacle. It has changed my life forever, yet I continue to be in awe of the everyday life that I have lived. The kitchen, the worship rooms, the stainless steel utensils, the billboards and the advertisements – my small-town existence was grabbed by the collar and changed forever.